OUT IN THE MIDDAY SUN
The Paintings of NOEL COWARD

—— Sheridan Morley ——

Phaidon · Christie's
Oxford

Phaidon · Christie's Limited, Littlegate House,
St. Ebbe's Street, Oxford OX1 1SQ
First published 1988
Introduction and captions © Phaidon · Christie's
    Limited 1988
Noël Coward lyrics, poems, autobiographies and
    diaries © the Estate of Noël Coward

British Library Cataloguing in Publication Data
Morley, Sheridan, 1941–
    Out in the midday sun : the paintings of
    Noel Coward
    1. English painting. Coward, Noel, 1899–1973
    I. Title II. Coward, Noel, 1899–1973
    759.2

ISBN 0–7148–8060–4

Printed and bound in England by Butler and Tanner
Limited, Frome

C O N T E N T S

Sheridan Morley would like to thank Graham Payn for his constant help and advice, and Graham Southern together with the staff at Christie's and Phaidon, without all of whom this book would not have been remotely possible.

Two Nuns (right)

At twelve noon
The natives swoon
And no further work is done.
But mad dogs and Englishmen
Go out in the midday sun.

(*Words and Music*, 1932)

Noël painting in his studio at Goldenhurst
Farm, Kent.

OUT IN THE MIDDAY SUN

Twenty years ago, when I was writing the first biography of Sir Noël Coward at his invitation, he asked me to spend one or two weekends at the chalet above Montreux in Switzerland which was his last European home. There I expected, and rightly, to find all his manuscripts and screenplays and family scrapbooks and the letters and the diaries and the sheet music and the records and the notebooks, and even to meet a few of the old friends and colleagues whom he knew I would need if I were ever to get the book finished.

What I didn't expect to find, and indeed only came across because I was wandering around the house one afternoon trying vaguely to work out the extent to which a novice biographer was also supposed to be a sort of private detective, was a room off the hall entirely filled from floor to ceiling with twenty years of his paintings.

Curiously, none of the paintings seemed to be of Switzerland, and only a very few were of the English country homes in Kent where he had spent most of the first fifty years of his life (see pages 26 and 32). Instead, they were mostly vivid seascapes and shorescapes of Jamaica, reminiscent perhaps of a sun-drenched Lowry or Hockney, and in talking to Noël about them it became immediately evident that they represented the lasting passion and hobby of the previous two decades. It wasn't, however, until his lifelong friend and the chief executor of his estate, Graham Payn, decided to put the paintings on sale for charity in the February of 1988, fifteen years after Coward's death, that any idea could be formed of their commercial value.

In his lifetime, Noël always reserved his own paintings as first-night or birthday gifts for friends, allowing only one or two to go for the very occasional charity auction and fearing, as he once wrote, that a kind of 'celebrity snobbism' might otherwise make them valued more for their autograph than for their intrinsic worth. When therefore the experts at Christie's came to estimate their value for the sale, they had very little precedent to work on and it was generally reckoned that thirty or so paintings would gross around £300,000.

In fact, they went for a grand total of £786,000 in one short sale, thereby happily vindicating Noël's own diary estimate that 'compared to the pretentious muck in some London galleries . . . my amateur efforts appear brilliant.' But what matters about these Coward paintings, apart from the fact that they and some which were not in the sale have been gathered here in one volume before vanishing into private collections, is that they reflect his delight in eventually arriving, from a rainsoaked South London childhood, at the place in the sun which is (as I have suggested in the caption quotations) the escapist theme of so many of his plays and songs and poems.

When Coward died in 1973 he was as old as the century and its most constant, if often controversial, showbusiness reflection, jack of all its entertainment trades and master of most. He left behind him over fifty plays, twenty-five films as writer, director or star, hundreds of songs, a ballet, two autobiographies, a thirty-year diary, a novel, several volumes of short stories and countless poems, sketches and recordings, not to mention the memories of three generations of playgoers on both sides of the Atlantic for whom he remained the most ineffably elegant and ubiquitous of entertainers.

But the paintings suggest that for Noël there was always a world elsewhere, and that world was usually Jamaica. He first discovered the island at the end of the war, staying at a house called Goldeneye where Ian Fleming wrote the first of his James Bond books and which Noël, a somewhat uneasy tenant, rapidly rechristened Golden Eye, Nose and Throat (see page 42). But he soon found his own home at Blue Harbour (see page 50) and it was there, or at the retreat he built above it at Firefly (see pages 68–9) that he did most of his best work as an artist, concentrating on local scenes and characters or else on those matchstick figures on distant golden beaches against clear blue skies.

When I had finished my biography, *A Talent to Amuse,* and coincidentally seen him return from a kind of postwar exile to a London where he was knighted at the time of his seventieth birthday and transformed almost overnight from an unfashionable writer of long-lost drawing room comedies to the grand old man of the British theatre, Noël sent me a seascape on which two tiny figures can be seen making their way across a beach (see page 33). 'You have to imagine' he wrote, 'that you are seeing them through a telescope, as that is the only way I can ever manage to paint people.'

Precisely when Noël first started to paint is unclear, though working on a picture album (*Noël Coward and His Friends,* 1979) years after his death, I did come across a number of amusing caricatures as well as a garish watercolour of Pavlova (see page 9) and one of Nell Gwyn (actually it could have been the Scarecrow from *The Wizard of Oz,* but he had firmly written 'Nell Gwyn' beneath it) signed by Noël at the age of ten and lovingly stored in a trunk by his mother. He then seems to have abandoned painting at the easel until the early 1930s when, as his secretary and friend Cole Lesley recalled, 'he began again, painting from time to time in watercolours, usually seascapes with ships in sepia or low-toned keys; rather naive but, as in everything he attempted, with a style of his own.'

The watercolours continued throughout the 1930s, usually painted at Goldenhurst in Kent on the rare weekends when he wasn't either in rehearsal or working on a new score. Then, one Sunday, he drove over to Chartwell to visit Winston Churchill with whom he maintained a long if occasionally rather edgy friendship and,

This painting of Anna Pavlova was done by
Noël as a boy.

noted Lesley, 'by the end of that Sunday Sir Winston had commanded him to stop painting in watercolours and work only in oils. Noël came back converted.'

From then on, throughout the late 1940s and into the 50s and 60s, Noël would paint whenever possible at his English, Swiss and above all Jamaican homes, insisting that friends should abandon their canasta and crosswords to join him in what became the most favourite and time-consuming of all his non-theatrical pastimes.

'He got off to a flying start', remembered Lesley, 'using oils exactly as he had used his watercolours and producing a perfectly lovely seascape in misty, pastel tones with a woman in red leading a small dog' (see page 23).

Advice was sought from several friends, not least the fashion designer Edward Molyneux, and the artist Derek Hill (who later painted one of the best portraits of Coward (see page 11)), and the writer Clemence Dane who recommended 'courage and attack'.

But it was really in Jamaica, where he made a winter home for several years, that he achieved his best work: 'not representational', as Cole Lesley wrote, 'but somehow catching the essential spirit and the many moods of that lovely island. It is true to say that all those countless hours he spent at his easel were among the most happy and carefree of his entire life.'

Noël himself was, as usual, the sharpest critic of his own work: writing in his 1955 diary, he noted, 'my paintings have a sense of colour and design, and do at least convey a fantasised impression of Jamaica; but as yet I am still at a stage where I break rules without really having learned them.'

Now that we at last have the chance to look at some of Coward's later work out in the midday sun, what do the paintings actually tell us about him? Certainly they convey his passion for sea and sand and sunshine, and the discovery of Jamaica as an island in the sun far from the bitter cold and damp of the English winters that he decided to leave behind him after the war. But to understand the truth about Noël, you have to go back to the very beginning, to a childhood far removed from the cocktails and laughter and what-comes-after image of the elegant figure in the silk dressing-gown with the clenched cigarette-holder.

Coward was born on 16 December 1899, just before the last Christmas of the last century (hence the name Noël). The second son of an unsuccessful piano tuner and a doting, ambitious backstage mother, he grew up in suburban, middle-class South London amid genteel poverty: 'I did not gnaw kippers' heads in the gutter as Gertie Lawrence always quite untruthfully claimed that she did,' he once wrote, 'nor was my first memory the crunch of carriage wheels in the drive, because we hadn't got a drive.'

When he was ten, his mother answered an advertisement in the *Daily Mirror* calling for child actors, and a few months later he was on stage at the Crystal Palace in a play called *The Goldfish* with what was memorably billed as 'a cast of wonder children'. By 1912 he was Slightly in *Peter Pan* (it was the critic Kenneth Tynan who later noted that he was to be Wholly in it forever afterwards) and he then settled, like his beloved Gertrude Lawrence, into the First War life of a moderately successful child actor. In his own view he was, 'when washed and smarmed down a bit passably attractive, but also one of the worst boy actors ever inflicted upon the paying public.'

Nevertheless he survived, and by 1917 was already making his first film, *Hearts of the World,* for D. W. Griffith which starred both Lillian and Dorothy Gish. There followed a brief and unhappy time in the army, another five years in the theatre and a disastrous trip to Broadway where, though falling rapidly in love with the energy and pace of the American theatre, he signally failed to sell any of the comedies or songs he had already written.

But then, in 1924 at the Everyman Theatre in Hampstead, came literally overnight the triumph of *The Vortex,* a play about drug addiction written at a time when even alcoholism was scarcely mentioned on the British stage. The almost equal amounts of interest, indignation, publicity, admiration and box-office cash generated by a play which

One of his first tutors, Derek Hill, painting Noël's portrait. Noël complained about the work: 'My eyes are too close together'.

Noël Coward first visited Jamaica in 1944
and was to return to the island throughout his
life.

Noël had written, directed and starred in (he also painted several of its sets), meant that at the age of twenty-four he went from being a mildly unsuccessful playwright, actor and composer to being the hottest theatrical figure in the West End – a change so rapid that even he took several months and a nervous breakdown to come to terms with it all:

'I was photographed and interviewed and photographed again. In the street. At my piano. With my dear old mother. Without my dear old mother. And on one occasion sitting up in bed looking like a heavily-doped Chinese illusionist. This last photograph did me a certain amount of harm: people glancing at it assumed that I was undoubtedly a weedy sensualist in the last stages of physical and moral disintegration, and that they had

Noël painting at Firefly Hill, Port Maria,
Jamaica, 1961. He wore gloves because of an
allergy to turpentine, and used a medium called
casein.

The studio at Goldenhurst where Noël began to paint. The wings hanging on the wall travelled with him from Kent through Bermuda to his final home at Les Avants in Switzerland, as did his piano, signed photographs and chair.

better hurry off to see me in my play before my inevitable demise placed that faintly macabre pleasure beyond their reach.'

There followed, in a rapid mid-1920s succession, such hits as *Fallen Angels, Hay Fever* and the revue *On With The Dance,* all of which ran simultaneously with *The Vortex* in London, a quadruple feat only elsewhere achieved in this century by Alan Ayckbourn and Somerset Maugham. Then came a year or two of total critical reversal, when boos greeted *Sirocco* and Noël was actually spat at in the street by irate theatregoers who felt his subsequent work had betrayed their initial enthusiasm.

But by 1929 Coward had started on his period of greatest success: within the next two years came *Private Lives,* the operetta *Bitter-Sweet* and the historical epic *Cavalcade,* so that by 1931 the Boy Wonder of the Twenties ('Destiny's Tot' as Aleck Woollcott once christened him) had settled into an altogether more stable pattern of theatrical success, one which was characterized by the partnership he had formed with Gertrude Lawrence.

For her he had written many of his best songs, as well as *Private Lives* itself, redolent of Riviera balconies, filled with the potency of cheap music, and shot through with the sadness of a couple who could live neither together nor apart, a couple who were in so many incidental ways Noël and Gertie themselves. Six years later they played together again in the nine short plays that made up his *Tonight at 8.30,* including of course the one that was to live on as a classic film of lost love, *Brief Encounter.*

Between those two towering landmarks of their stage relationship, Noël also found the time to write *Design For Living* for the Lunts, *Words and Music* for the producer Charles Cochran, *Conversation Piece* for Yvonne Printemps and, soon afterwards, *Operette* for Fritzi Massary:

'Throughout the 1930s in fact', he wrote, 'I was a highly publicised and irritatingly successful figure, much in demand; the critical laurels that had been so confidently predicted for me in my twenties never graced my brow, and I was forced to console myself with the bitter palliative of box-office success, which I enjoyed very much indeed.'

With the coming of the Second War, Noël went into propaganda work in France and then a series of charity, troop and concert tours, only to return in 1945 to a London that had changed out of all recognition. The West End theatre was no longer his kind of theatre, Gertrude Lawrence was married in America and soon to die tragically young, and there seemed less and less to keep him around a Shaftesbury Avenue that had moved far away from the prewar grace and elegance and wit of his own best work.

In America, and specifically in cabaret at Las Vegas, he found an altogether new audience, known to him as NesCafé Society, and through such movies as *Our Man in Havana,* through Broadway musicals like *Sail Away*

and *The Girl Who Came to Supper*, and through his short stories, he came to discover a world far removed from the old West End.

Jamaica, too, was a part of that new world, and it was one from which Coward only really returned at the very end of his life, when a National Theatre revival of *Hay Fever* (commissioned at Kenneth Tynan's suggestion by Laurence Olivier, who had been with Coward in the first *Private Lives*) suddenly brought him back into focus at home. Seasons of his work on stage, television and at the National Film Theatre followed soon afterwards, and a perpetually blithe spirit had come back into his own. Since that time his work has scarcely ever been out of revival, and the recent Christie's sale coincided with major new productions of *Easy Virtue, Bitter-Sweet* and *The Vortex*, all rediscovered from the 1920s.

But Noël himself knew that by the time of his seventieth birthday and the knighthood in 1969 it was almost all over: 'it's terrifying', he wrote to a friend, 'how little time there is left. Every day now is a dividend and there is still so much I want to do. But my life until now has left me with no permanent regrets of any kind. I don't look back in anger, nor indeed in anything approaching even mild rage; I rather look back in pleasure and amusement. As for death, it holds no fear for me, provided it is not going to be a painfully lingering affair.'

It wasn't: he died suddenly in Jamaica on March 26th 1973, after a few more tranquil winters spent painting in the sunshine; 'for I believe, that since my life began, the most I've had is just a talent to amuse'. He lies buried in the garden of his last home there, and a reminder of that talent is inscribed on his memorial stone in Westminster Abbey.

Thanks to Graham Payn's decision to put these paintings in the public arena for the first time and to use their profits to benefit Noël's own favourite theatrical charities, we have other and more colourful reminders. Not that Noël himself ever took his painting too seriously, though I think he would have been delighted and amused, and maybe a little amazed, by the sudden and worldwide burst of interest that surrounded the Christie's sale and by the five-figure sums fetched by some of his Jamaican landscapes.

For the man who once talked of his 'touch and Gauguin' period and told Cole Lesley (then himself going through an Impressionist phase), 'Monet, Monet, Monet, that's all you ever think about', was not above painting over the canvases of early Victorian pictures he bought in junkshops, so that his own work would have ready-made frames. It was left to Cole Lesley to wonder whether the originals might now have been of even greater value.

Yet, as Graham Payn recalls:

'Painting played a central role in Noël's creative life. In fact wherever he and Coley and I travelled in the world, whether in Jamaica or Switzerland or Italy or in the heart of England, and whatever was occupying the main focus of his attention, he always used painting as both a relaxation and an inspiration. His mind was never idle while he was wielding a brush, and frequently he would use the peace of his studio to work out in his mind the more complex aspects of his theatrical work. One might almost suggest that without his painting, much of his playwriting and songwriting would have progressed far less smoothly.'

It does not require an art critic, and I am indeed not one, to remark that there is something highly theatrical about almost all of Noël's paintings: Lowry and Hockney might be the most immediate touchstones among painters, but there are strong overtones of both Oliver Messel and Cecil Beaton in his work, and both of course were scenic

A rare example of a poster designed by Noël
for the 1961 premiere of *Sail Away.*

18

Bonard Productions
in association with Charles Russell *presents*

Noël Coward's

new musical comedy

Sail Away

starring

Elaine Stritch   Jean Fenn

with

James Hurst   Margalo Gillmore   Alice Pearce   Patricia Harty   Grover Dale
Carroll McComas   William Hutt   Charles Braswell   Betty Jane Watson   Evelyn Russell

Production Designed by OLIVER SMITH
Costumes Designed by HELENE PONS *and* OLIVER SMITH
Lighting by Peggy Clark
Musical Direction and Dance Arrangements by Peter Matz
Orchestrations by Irwin Kostal   *Vocal Arrangements by* Fred Werner

Musical Numbers and Dances Staged by JOE LAYTON
Book, Music, Lyrics and Direction by NOËL COWARD

COLONIAL THEATRE BOSTON MATS. WED. & SAT.   **WED. AUG. 9** THRU **SAT. SEPT. 2**

Printed by Artcraft Litho. & Ptg. Co., Inc. N. Y. C.   491

designers. Many of Noël's landscapes look like stage sets for some sun-baked operetta, and his vivid colouring is highly theatrical (see page 24). But though he designed one or two programme-covers for charity matinees, and we do have here one example of a rare poster he painted for his musical *Sail Away* (see page 19), he in fact designed none of his own shows, leaving that task almost always to his lifelong friend Gladys Calthrop.

Yet, as Graham Payn also recalls:

'painting was so important to Noël that for long periods of his life it was something more than a relaxation from the theatre or the typewriter: he became almost fanatical about it, and if a picture was going especially well he would do anything to be able to carry on with it while the mood was obviously right. He would skip tea, turn down the pre-dinner drink and frequently would carry on late into the evening. Light didn't really matter to him: electricity was just as good as daylight, for he always painted indoors. He had tried the open air, but conditions outdoors can be pretty uncomfortable. I remember one disastrous expedition when we both thought we would go out and paint the view over the bay: but with the wind, dust, flies, bees and bugs both irritating us and getting stuck in the wet paint it was simply tortuous, so after a few minutes we gave up the attempt and fled back indoors to the civilized cool of the studio. But although Noël always painted at home, the subjects were all based on real places and recalled from his wonderful memory.'

For anyone who knows or wants to know about Coward, some of the clues are here in the paintings: a sense of style and simplicity, a love of life, a brisk kind of humour and a constant reminder of the bold colouring of the toy theatres of his own childhood. Much of the world for which Coward stands as a showbusiness symbol has already been blown to extinction, but he was his own invention and contribution to a golden period of theatrical and musical history which he had himself helped to define. 'Anyone who cannot see that', as John Osborne once noted, 'should leave the theatre.' As for the rest of us, we should maybe now gather around Noël's paintings, the last great undiscovered aspect of that remarkably versatile talent to amuse.

'THE PAINTINGS'

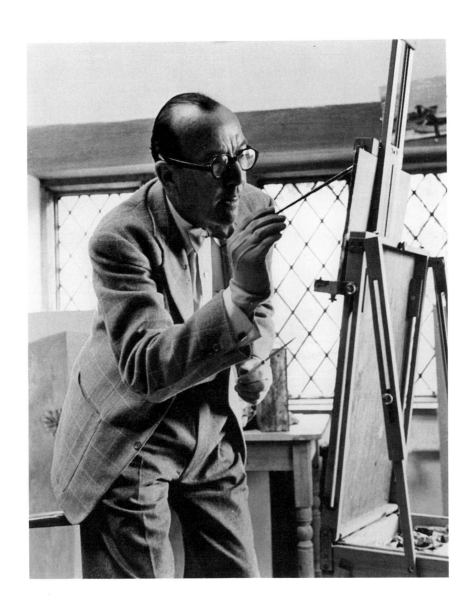

The Sea-front

'A room with a view — and you,
With no one to worry us,
No one to hurry us — through
This dream we've found,
We'll gaze at the sky — and try
To guess what it's all about,
Then we will figure out — why
The world is round.'

(*This Year of Grace*, 1928)

Lady in Red (right)

The painting of the woman in the red dress with the dog was Noël's first attempt at oils.

23

Trees on the Edge of a Lake

'When I left England first, long years ago,
I looked back at the swiftly fading shore
And suddenly, quite without warning, knew
That I was sad at leaving. It is true
That I was on a holiday, no war
Was dragging me abroad, but even so
How strange it was. How strange it is, this strong,
Deep-rooted feeling for one's native land.
When is it born? Why should it come to flower
So inconveniently just at the hour
Of parting? I have grown to understand
In later years, after so many long,
Far journeyings. But on that distant day
When first I felt that unexpected, gentle
Tug at my heart, I tried to keep at bay
Such foolishness and, as I turned away,
Laughed at myself for being sentimental.'

Like much of his work this painting has a bold fore-
ground design with the quality of a stage set –
Coward's landscapes could often have been scenery.

The Pond at Goldenhurst Farm, Kent

'I decided that I am going to . . . go back to Goldenhurst. It is my own land and much quieter. I shall
miss the sea and the ships but I shall have the Marsh and the trees, the orchard and the croquet lawn.'
(*Diary*, July 2nd 1951)

Noël bought Goldenhurst Farm in Kent in 1928 and sold it in 1955. It was his country and family
home except during the war, when it was occupied by the army.

Fisherman in a Boat and Bathers on the Edge of a Lake

When your life seems too difficult to rise above,
Sail away — sail away.
When your heart feels as dreary as a worn-out glove,
Sail away — sail away.
But when soon or late
You recognize your fate
That will be your great, great day,
On the wings of the morning with your own true love,
Sail Away — sail away — sail away!

(*Ace of Clubs*, 1950)

Romney Marsh (right)

Given by Noël to his lifelong friend
the actress Joyce Carey, who played
in many of his comedies from *Easy Virtue*
across thirty years to *South Sea Bubble*.

Looking Out to Sea

'This was another holiday, another escape, another change of rhythm. In the months before me I should have a little breathing space in which to weigh values, reassemble experience, analyse motives and endeavour to balance the past and present against the future . . . when I came up on deck there was no England left. Nothing but sea and sky'.

(*Present Indicative*, 1937)

The Cliffs above St Margaret's Bay

'Drove down to White Cliffs in the Ford brake: as usual the weather was wet and bleak until we passed Canterbury, then the sun came out and by the time we reached St Margaret's Bay it was like summer . . . that night there was a full moon making a highway across the sea, the South Foreland was flashing and there were ships far out in the Channel wearing coloured lights. An evening of enchantment: I know this is going to be a happy house.' (*Diary*, October 18 1945)

Noël lived at White Cliffs in St Margaret's Bay from 1945 to 1951 while Goldenhurst was being restored after the war.

Two Figures on a Beach (right)

Given to Sheridan Morley after he had written *A Talent to Amuse* in 1969, the first Coward biography.

Venice

Last Wednesday on the Piazza
Near San Marco's trecento Duomo
I observed una grassa ragazza
With a thin, Middle Western uomo.

He was swatting a piccola mosca
She was eating a chocolate gelato
While an orchestra played (from *La Tosca*)
A flat violin obbligato.

They stared at a dusty piccione
They spoke not a single parola
She ordered some Te con limone
He ordered an iced Coca-Cola.

And while the tramanto del sole
Set fire to the Grande Canale
She scribbled haphazard parole
On glazed cartoline postale.

(*Collected Verse*)

Windmill, Lighthouse and White Cliffs (left)

An imaginary scene but perhaps inspired by the Kent coastline near his White Cliffs.

Snow Scene

Skier (right)

'Fair though the faces and places I've known,
When the dream is ended and passion has flown
I travel alone.
Free from love's illusion, my heart is my own:
I travel alone.'

(*I Travel Alone*, 1935)

Portofino

The Harbour, Portofino (right)

'Today we are leaving with regret. Portofino has been by far the nicest part of our holiday. We have swum and sunbathed and painted pictures. We have eaten delicious dinners at Pitsforo's on the Port. We have gossiped with Truman Capote and have been entertained on a hideous Edwardian yacht by the Henry Luces and Maggie Case. We have laughed a great deal with Rex and Lilli and revelled in talking our own language again. In fact it has been lovely and I most firmly intend to come again.' (*Diary*, September 1953)

Blue Hills, Jamaica

Tropical Coastline (right)

'My first view of Jamaica was from an altitude of about eight thousand feet. The morning was cloudless and the island was discernible from many miles away. Now, remembering that moment nine years ago, my mind becomes choked with clichés. "Had I but known then . . .", "Little did I dream . . .", "If only I could have foreseen" but of course I didn't know or dream or foresee how familiar that particular sight would become, how many times in the future I was destined to see these green hills and blue mountains rising out of the sea.' (*Future Indefinite*, 1954)

The Sunken Garden, Goldeneye, Jamaica

'Ah, Goldeneye! Sedate, historic pile
Haven of peace for those in dire distress
Welcome oasis in a wilderness
Of dreadful rumour and most wild surmise
Dear sanctuary, screened from prying eyes
Sylvan retreat, impregnable and kind
Giver of solace to the weary mind
To you, to you we fly to rest awhile
Here to this gracious home, this grateful harbour
Wrought, not by Vanburgh, but Scovell and Barber.'

(Collected Verse)

Noël rented Ian Fleming's house Goldeneye at Oracabessa in Jamaica in 1948. Subsequently he decided to make Jamaica his winter home and began to look for a suitable site on which to build a house. This was found a few miles along the coast at Port Maria and Noël decided to name his property Blue Harbour.

People before a Coastal Inlet, Jamaica (right)

Hillside Church

Sortie de l'Eglise (right)
(Reproduced by gracious permission of Her Majesty Queen Elizabeth The Queen Mother)

'Let's leave the milk-bar snacks,
Perms and breakfast foods
To those girls in plastic macs,
Slacks and pixie hoods.
Let's start today
For somewhere gayer, warmer, dryer,
England's too damp for us
Let's fly away.'

(*Let's Fly Away*, 1949)

Red Interior

Given by Graham Payn to Elizabeth Taylor to give to Richard Burton on the first night of a revival of
Private Lives, New York, 1983.

Red Roof and Tropical Coastline (left)

Bathers on a Jetty

'They sing from morning till night. They weave away and make the most lovely waste-paper baskets and never stop having scads of entrancing children who swim before they can walk and have enormous melting eyes like saucers. And whenever they feel a bit peckish, all they have to do is to nip a breadfruit off a tree or snatch a yam out of the ground . . . they hunt and dive and swim and fish and make the most wonderful things with their hands.' (*South Sea Bubble*, 1956)

Purple Hills (right)

Harbour

'We also saw a double rainbow and for a few moments the whole land was bathed in a pinky gold light. We drove home and I thought of a name for the house, Blue Harbour. It is a good name because it sounds nice and really describes the view. The house is to be built against the hill on different levels. It will be ready in December. I am very happy.' (*Diary*, 1948)

Noël built Blue Harbour in 1948.

People outside a Mediterranean Church

'Do I believe in God?
Well yes, I suppose, in a sort of way.
It's really terribly hard to say.
I'm sure that there must be of course
Some kind of vital, motive force,
Some power that holds the winning card
Behind life's ambiguous façades
But whether you think me odd or not
I can't decide if it's God or not.'

(Not Yet The Dodo, 1967)

People in an Italian Street

'Do I believe in God?
I can't say No and I can't say Yes
To me it's anybody's guess
But if all's true that we once were told
Before we grew wise and sad and old
When finally Death rolls up our eyes
We'll find we're in for a big surprise.'

(*Not Yet The Dodo*, 1967)

Purple Interior

Workmen Building Swimming-Pool at Blue Harbour (right)

When Blue Harbour was built, Coward was disappointed with the result. The house was supposed to have been constructed layer by layer to follow the lie of the hillside, but instead it rose up severely against the skyline. The stark effect of this was not improved by the fact that the house was painted white and all the surrounding foliage had been removed.

Palm Trees and Hut

'When the storm clouds are riding through a winter sky,
Sail Away – sail away.
When the love-light is fading in your sweetheart's eye
Sail Away – sail away.
When you feel your song is orchestrated wrong,
Why should you prolong
Your stay?
When the wind and the weather blow your dreams sky high
Sail Away – sail away.'

(*Ace of Clubs,* 1950)

The Gardener at Firefly

A rare example of a Coward portrait – he considered himself better at landscapes. He is working on
this picture in the photograph opposite.

Pomp and Circumstance book jacket, designed by Coward, 1960

Samolo Bay (left)

'Samolo is the largest of an archipelago of thirty-four islands, seven of which are uninhabited and a few privately owned. The whole group was discovered by Captain Evangelus Cobb in the year 1786. They are of volcanic origin and situated in the South-Western Pacific. Latitude 18 degrees north and longitude, if you are still interested, 175 degrees west.' (*Pomp and Circumstance,* 1960)

Samolo was, in fact, a fictional tropical island that Noël used as the setting for his comedy *South Sea Bubble,* the operetta *Pacific 1860,* a short story *Solali,* and his novel *Pomp and Circumstance.*

Mooring a Boat, Blue Harbour, Port Maria, Jamaica

'I saw no shadow on the sea,
No voices called to me,
My life was free,
How could I open wide my arms
To the paradise around me
When no love had ever found me
The key?'

(*Pacific 1860*, 1946)

The Red Sailing Boat

'A different sky
New worlds to gaze upon,
The strange excitement of an unfamiliar shore,
One more goodbye,
One more illusion gone,
Just cut your losses
And begin once more.'

(Sail Away, 1960)

On the Jamaican Coast

'We discussed over drinks the possibility of building a shack isolated on this island and how wonderful it would be to have such an idyllic bolt-hole to return to when life became too frustrating.

The climate is so equable and lovely. There are no insects or pests. There is, above all, peace. I am thinking very seriously about this. Something tells me the time has come to make a few plans for escape in the future.' (*Diary*, 1948)

A Road in Jamaica

Jamaican Mountains (right)

'When I'm feeling dreary and blue,
I'm only too
Glad to be left alone,
Dreaming of a place in the sun.
When day is done,
Far from a telephone;
Bustle and the weary crowd
Make me want to cry out loud,
Give me something peaceful and grand
Where all the land
Slumbers in monotone.'

(*This Year of Grace*, 1928)

Noël standing on his terrace at Firefly

'It is enchanting; an old stone house, roofless but with thick walls and the most fabulous view. I want to buy it, ostensibly as a writing retreat but really with a view to making it lovely for the future, letting or selling Blue Harbour and living in it.' (*Diary*, May 1948)

The Terrace, Firefly, Port Maria, Jamaica

Noël never did let or sell Blue Harbour but increasingly he did use Firefly, the house he built near the ruins of what had once been the buccaneering Captain Sir Henry Morgan's 'look-out', as a writing retreat.

People on the Quay

Jamaican Road (right)

'Home again at Blue Harbour and everything unbelievably lovely. The garden has grown so fast that it is quite unrecognisable. The air is warm and soft and so is the sea. I have fallen in love with the place all over again and this time next year I shall install myself for six months instead of seven weeks. I dread the time passing already . . . I am alone in the guest house with all my things round me. It is utterly peaceful and tomorrow I shall be fifty and I couldn't care less.' (*Diary*, December 1949)

The sombre, bold tones of the early work are now expanded into Jamaican crowd scenes of more courageous compositions combining vivid colours with daring design.

Unloading on the Quay, Jamaica

Loading a Cargo Ship (right)

'No more waiting through empty years,
Pearls and diamonds in place of tears,
When my ship comes home.
Through the world I'll roam.
Open skies above me,
Someone dear to love me,
When my ship comes home.'

(*London Calling*, 1923)

Market Scene

Boy Peeling an Orange (right)

'Jamaica's an island surrounded by sea
(Like Alderney, Guernsey and Sark are)
It's wise not to drive with exuberant glee
Where large barracuda and shark are.
The reefs are entrancing; the water is clear,
The colouring couldn't be dreamier
But one coral scratch and you may spend a year
In bed with acute septicemia.'

(*Collected Verse*)

On a Beach in Jamaica

'In tropical climes there are certain times of day
When all the citizens retire
To tear their clothes off and perspire.
It's one of those rules that the greatest fools obey,
Because the sun is much too sultry
And one must avoid its ultry-violet ray.'

(*Words and Music*, 1932)

Under a Palm Tree, Jamaica

'The world is wide and when my day is done
I shall at least have travelled free,
Led by this wanderlust that turns my eyes to far horizons.
Though time and tide won't wait for anyone,
There's one illusion left for me
And that's the happiness I've known alone.'

(1935)

The View from Firefly

'. . . laughter learnt of friends, and gentleness, in a
Jamaican heaven'. (1949)

Noël died at Firefly on March 26th 1973 and is buried in
its garden.

INDEX

ACKNOWLEDGEMENTS

The publishers are grateful to the following for their help in locating and lending paintings: Joyce Carey, Kenneth Cleveland, Louise Corrigan, Michael Cox, Barry Day, Miss Radie Harris, Mrs Joan Hirst, Jerry Hogan, Geoffrey Johnson, Her Majesty The Queen Mother, R. H. V. Moorhead, Sheridan Morley, Graham Payn, Graham Southern, Martin Tickner, Mr P. Woollard.

Quotations from the following titles, all of which are available in paperback, are by the kind permission of the publisher: Collected Verse, Noël Coward, Methuen, London and New York; The Lyrics, Noël Coward, Methuen, London; The Autobiographies of Noël Coward, Methuen, London; Diaries of Noël Coward, Weidenfeld and Nicolson, London.

Photographic acknowledgements: Cecil Beaton, Sotheby's p. 2; Guy Gravett pp. 1, 2, 6, 14–15, 17, 21, 27; Jamaican Tourist Office p. 12; Geoffrey Johnson p. 13; Peter Marshall, Toronto p. 3; Mark Swain p. 2; Horst Tappé, Camera Press p. 3, back cover.